© original edition 2010, paperback edition 2017, Prestel Verlag, Munich · London · New York
A member of Verlagsgruppe Random House GmbH
Neumarkter Strasse 28 · 81673 Munich

Prestel Publishing Ltd.
14-17 Wells Street
London W1T 3PD

Prestel Publishing
900 Broadway, Suite 603
New York, NY 10003

In respect to links in the book, the Publisher expressly notes that no illegal content was discernible on the linked sites at the time the links were created. The Publisher has no influence at all over the current and future design, content or authorship of the linked sites. For this reason the Publisher expressly disassociates itself from all content on linked sites that has been altered since the link was created and assumes no liability for such content.

Front cover: Victor Vasarely, *Zebra* (detail, photo: bridgeman)
Frontispiece: *Blue Sky* (Warren Edward Johnson), *Tunnel Vision*, 1975. Wall painting in Columbia, South Carolina

Picture Credits: The pictures in this book were graciously made available by the museums and collections mentioned, or have been taken from the publisher's archive with exception of: ADAGP, banque d'images p. 41, 78 above; akg-images p. 73; Alex MacNaughton p. 40; artothek p. 46, 54; bpk p. 30; bridgeman p. 12, 28; Magic Eye Inc. p. 26; Robert Silvers p. 63; Scala p. 32; Schwäbisches Bauernhofmuseum, Illerbeuren p. 66-67; ThinkFun Inc. p. 81.

Library of Congress Control Number: 2017947216
A CIP catalogue record for this book is available from the British Library.

Translated by: Cynthia Hall
Copyedited by: Brad Finger
Editorial direction: Doris Kutschbach, Larissa Spicker
Design and layout: Michael Schmölzl, agenten.und.freunde, Munich
Production: Corinna Pickart
Origination: Reproline Genceller
Printing and Binding: DZS Grafik, d.o.o., Ljubljana
Paper: Profimatt

Verlagsgruppe Random House FSC®N001967

Printed in Slowenia

ISBN 978-3-7913-7321-8

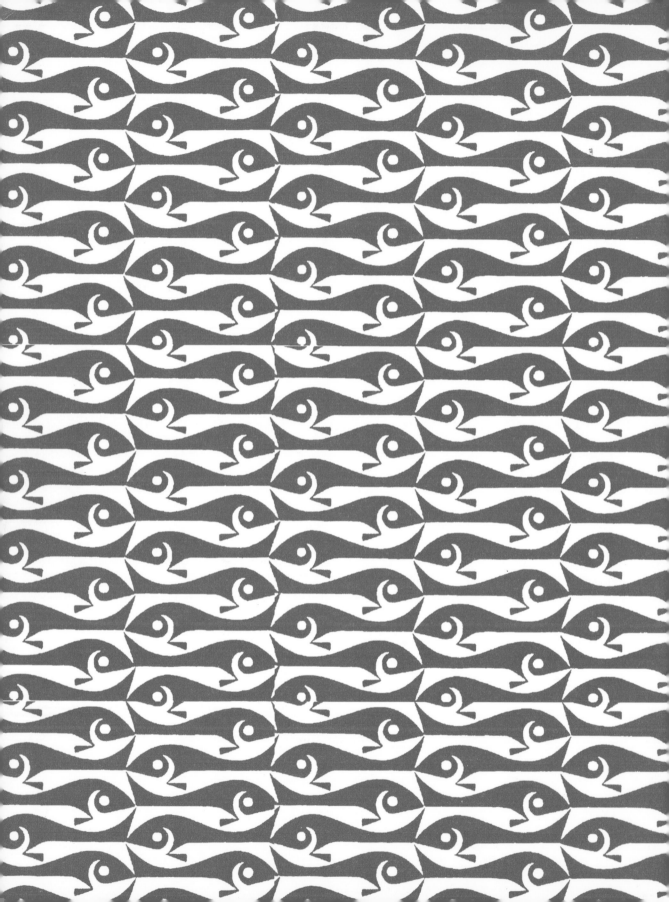

To Sebastian and Juliana

Silke Vry

Trick of the Eye

Art and Illusion

Prestel

Munich · London · New York

Contents

Follow these clues.

Don't be afraid of tricksters

Can you believe your eyes? Can you tell the difference between a painted object and a real one? Do you see a green field as green and a red wall as red?

Are you sure?

What you probably don't suspect is that our eyes—and we, too—are fooled all the time by the most incredible tricks. And we often don't even notice. It happens to us in nature (see page 13) and also, more than anywhere else, in art—not only in painting, but also in architecture!

Many artists are great masters of the art of deception. There's almost no one better at playing fantastic tricks on our powers of perception.

And there's no reason to worry. Unlike real con artists, artist tricksters can be fun!

So, open your eyes and experience the pleasures of deception …

muel van Hoogstraten,
odlibet (detail), 1666.
aatliche Kunsthalle, Karlsruhe

Domenico Remps (?), *Art Cabinet*, second half of the seventeenth century. Opificio delle Pietre Dure, Florence

Painters are liars!

And the best painters are the biggest liars…

This was the judgment made by an Italian sculptor more than 400 years ago about his painter colleagues. Why did he believe this?

Painters do nothing other than paint canvases with colors. In doing so, they create beautiful landscapes, pictures of people who seem full of life, and many other things that look amazing and real.

But if you run your hand over the flat canvas, you'll soon discover that it's all only an illusion! A picture is always a picture, no more and no less.

René Magritte,
The Treachery of Images, 1929.
Los Angeles County Museum of Art

A painted pipe is not really a pipe, but only a picture of one.

So the artist of this picture has written "This is not a pipe" underneath the pipe in his picture.

Sounds confusing … but it actually makes perfect sense, doesn't it?

Real or painted?

The history of art is the history of illusion.

For hundreds of years, artists often tried to achieve one thing: they wanted their pictures to reproduce reality as exactly as possible.

More than 2,000 years ago, two famous Greek painters—Zeuxis and Parrhasius—argued about which of them was the greatest artist, which one could paint nature more accurately. They agreed to a contest to decide the matter once and for all. The next time they met, they showed each other the pictures they had painted. Zeuxis unveiled his painting first. As soon as he did so, doves flew to his painting to peck at the grapes he had painted. The delighted Zeuxis was sure he had already won the contest. But then they had to take a look at Parrhasius' painting. Zeuxis asked his colleague if he might be allowed to open the curtain covering the painting. He reached out to touch it and, instead of feeling a curtain, his hand felt … the picture. The curtain was only painted!

So who do you think was the greater artist: Zeuxis or Parrhasius?

Read about it
on page
76.

Adriaen van der Spelt and Frans von Mieris, *Trompe-l'Oeil with Garland of Flowers and a Curtain*, 1658. The Art Institute, Chicago

Eye test for beginners

Original and deception …

An exact copy of nature—is there really any such thing?
Some photographs of real objects have been hidden among
these pictures of painted artworks. Can you find them?

Read about it
on page
76.

The trickster in the sky: nature shows the way!

Who would have thought that even nature can perform optical tricks and fool our eyes? It happens more often than you might think …

On a clear night with a full moon, you can see nature's most famous optical illusion: the "moon illusion." When the moon appears near the horizon or near a house or tree; it seems to be larger than when it appears high up in the sky. But if you take a picture with a camera, the very same low-lying moon would look much smaller.

Why is this? Even scientists are not entirely sure!

The moon is very far away from us. Seen from the Earth, it's hard to imagine just how large it is. When this heavenly body is high up in the night sky—surrounded by dark space and a few tiny stars—then it may seem relatively small to our eyes. But when seen next to a neighbor's house, on the other hand, the moon may seem large to us.

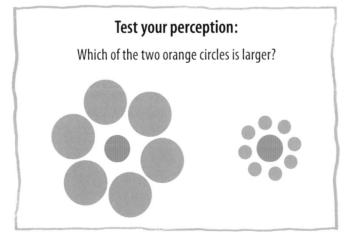

Test your perception:

Which of the two orange circles is larger?

Read about it on page 76.

Honoré Daumier,
Night of a Full Moon.
Illustration from the magazine
Le Charivari, 1844

The "moon illusion" can be observed not only with the moon but also with the sun. As soon as it sets and approaches the horizon, it appears incredibly large to us.

Vincent van Gogh, the painter of the picture to the right, depicted the sunset as he saw it with his eyes. If a photographer had photographed the same scene, the sun would look much smaller. The camera isn't fooled by nature's tricks!

Read about it on page 76.

Optical illusion: do it yourself

You can easily make an optical illusion yourself. You only need a camera. How does it work?

Did you know?

How is it possible that during an eclipse, the moon hides the sun, which is much larger?

a) It's an optical illusion.

b) It's because the sun is much further away from the Earth than the moon is.

c) Within the vastness of space, all heavenly bodies seem the same size.

Read about it on page 76.

Vincent van Gogh, *The Sower*, 1888. Rijksmuseum Vincent van Gogh, Amsterdam

What is the sky really like?

Not only do the sun and moon trick our eyes, but almost nothing in the sky is what it seems. Stars are not star-shaped in reality, and the sky is not actually blue! These are all optical illusions.

Do you want to know more?

It's alive! The illusion of deceptively real people

"It's alive! Look out, step aside! Here art comes alive and pictures leap from their frames ..."

For hundreds of years, many artists sought to make objects and people look lifelike—as if they might breathe, speak, and at any moment walk on their own power! Artists could even conjure up a lifelike being from a cold block of marble. Around 2,500 years ago, a sculptor created something unique using a pair of simple tricks. He carved a statue of a goddess, who was so beautiful and so lifelike that all the men who saw her fell in love with her.

There is a story about the Greek sculptor Pygmalion, in which he falls in love with one of his own statues. Aphrodite, the goddess of love, gave the sculpture life.

Franz von Stuck, *Pygmalion*, 1926. Private collection

Living faces

With the help of an optical illusion, you can recreate what the Greek sculptors achieved: awakening a work of art to life ...

Read about it on page 83.

re Borrell del Caso,
aping Criticism, 1874.
nco de Espana, Madrid

People who lived almost six hundred years ago were flabbergasted when they saw this picture for the first time. The painting is called an altarpiece, and it shows people and stories from the Bible. Everything seems deceptively real: the room, the statues, as well the winged angel and the other figures. The picture looks almost as lifelike as a photograph, as if a moment of reality had been captured in paint. But remember … photography was invented four hundred years after this picture was painted!

O

E

D

V

Read about it on page 76.

How does an artist paint the Holy Spirit?

Four details from the altarpiece appear above, each with its own letter. Can you find where these occur? If you sort them out from left to right, as they appear in the painting, the letters will spell out the name of a famous animal that represents the Holy Spirit—or the spirit of God. This creature appears over the head of Mary, the mother of Jesus, who is shown with crossed hands in the upper right part of the picture.

Hubert and Jan van Eyck, *Ghent Altarpiece*, 1432. St. Bavo, Ghent

Time for a break! There's sure to be a seat free soon ...

No, here we would have to wait a very long time. These two museum visitors are not getting up anytime soon, since they're both made of plastic ...

"Plastic"—not at all "fantastic"!

The artist who made these figures wanted them to look deceptively real, but he didn't really want to "fool" anyone with his plastic people. His art aimed at something different. He wanted to show people exactly as they are; complete with wrinkles, glasses, and ordinary clothes!

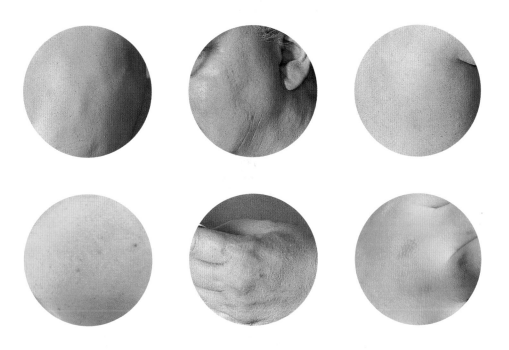

Real or not?
Two photos of "real" people have been mixed in with these details of the two "museum visitors" to the left. Can you find them?

Read about it on page 76.

Here's looking at you ...

It has been said that Leonardo da Vinci's mysterious Mona Lisa always gazes directly at her viewer, no matter where that viewer is in the room. Try it yourself. Is it true?

Portraits* by many other artists as well are said to have this curious quality. It makes the painted image of a person appear especially lifelike. But how does it happen? A picture can't move its eyes or turn its head …

* A portrait is a painting that represents a specific person.

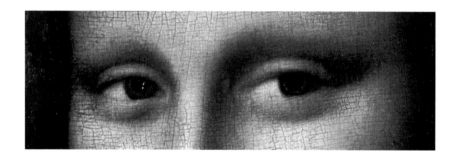

How do you think it happens?

a) It's not the portrait that looks at the viewer, but the viewer who looks at the portrait. The viewer only believes that his gaze is returned.

b) The painter created the picture in the mirror as a self-portrait, and that's why it looks so realistic

c) Mona Lisa is squinting, and she seems to steal a glance at the viewer.

d) There's a special art to it, which only very few artists have mastered.

Read about it on page 76.

Leonardo da Vi
Mona Lisa, around 15
Musée de Louvre, P

Jan Vermeer, *Girl with a Pearl Earring*, around 1665. Mauritshuis, Königliches Gemäldekabinett, the Hague

Just who is looking where?

The young lady in the picture to the left seems to be looking at you directly in the eyes, doesn't she

The trick with the glance

Look at the picture on the right. It's almost completely identical to the one on the left, with only one small change ... Most of the picture is shown in mirror-image. The eyes, however, are not shown as mirror images. They are completely unchanged. You can check this yourself by placing strips of paper over the faces, leaving only the eyes free.

Do the eyes still look at you?

Read about it on page 76.

But is she really looking at you?

What are you looking at?

It's incredible but true! You can make for yourself a nice little dragon that always keeps its eyes on you ... even though it never moves its head.

*Read about it
on page
81.*

Eye test for clever viewers

So, are you starting to get the picture? Then you'll surely find an explanation for these two strange pictures.

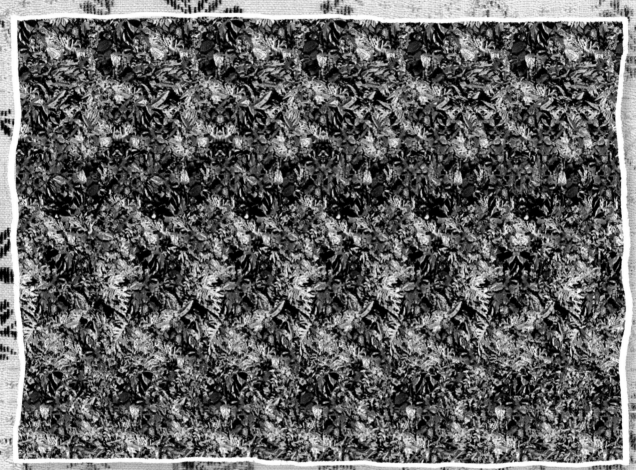

Read about it on page 77.

Magic eyes

Do you have two "magic eyes"? Try it out!

What do you have to do to see what's in this picture?

From fair to foul ...

Why is the picture of this pretty young lady upside down?
We should fix that right away ...
But wait a minute, maybe we should leave it like it is. Somehow, being upside
down seems to suit her better. Why?

*Read about it
on page
77.*

Samuel van Hoogstraten,
View of a Corridor, 1662.
Dyrham Park, Avon

Painters show perspective

"Come on in! Welcome! Don't be afraid of the dog, he doesn't bite. Walk right through, straight ahead, the other guests have already arrived …"

How nice it would be to accept the invitation and just walk down the seemingly endless hallway.

But once again, what you see is only a painting. It's as if the painter has opened a door and let us look through his own house!

The impression of "looking through" something in a painting is created only if the artist can paint in "perspective" and—like the painter here—knows a few optical tricks …

"Perspective" comes from the Latin "per-spicere," and it means "to look through."

It looks like someone's just discovered us, and is looking at us expectantly! But this too is one of the painter's tricks; he makes it seem as if we're in the middle of what's happening.

Who has perspective?

To paint in "perspective," of course, a painter has to know how perspective works.

The simplest rule of perspective is:

the further away an object is, the smaller it appears.

You would be quite astonished if this were not the case, and a person coming

towards you from a distance looked just as large as if he were right beside you.

Francesco di Giorgio Martini, *Architectural Veduta* (Ideal City), around 1490–1500.
Gemäldegalerie, Berlin (we cheated and added the three men to the picture)

**Read about it
on page
77.**

Big, bigger, biggest ...
Can you solve the riddle of the three funny men? Which of the three is the
largest, and which is the smallest?

Even more tricks!

If a painter wants to create the impression of almost endless depth on a canvas or other flat object, he or she has to know even more tricks than only the one of people and objects "getting smaller and smaller."

In this sketch, you can see the three figures once again. The one on the left is large, and the one on the right is smaller. There is nothing unusual about this, and there's nothing to indicate that one of the men is further away from you than the others.

But if you place the figures in front of a drawing of a wall, things suddenly look very different ...

For this exercise you need the drawing on page 80, as well as a pencil and a ruler. Now draw a line connecting point A with A, B with B, and so on. Make sure that you don't draw the lines through the figures, but make it look like the lines run behind them ...

How do the figures look when your drawing is done?

Often only a few lines that seem to recede—or move backwards—diagonally are enough to create the impression of space. For a moment, your eyes are fooled.

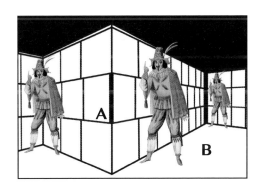

Which line seems longer to you, A or B?

Read about it on page 77.

A view into endless depth ...

Over time, the painter of the long hallway on page 28 perfected his "perspectives" more and more. He built peep-show cabinets for the viewer to look into, and painted their interiors with pictures. Through distortions of perspective and optical tricks, he made it seem like the viewer was looking into a real and endless space—which was much deeper than the actual cabinet …

Samuel van Hoogstraten,
*A Peepshow with Views of the
Interior of a Dutch House*, 1660.
National Gallery, London

Build a simple
perspective box!

*Read about it
on page
85.*

Parthenon, 5th century B.C. Acropolis, Athens

Why is the temple crooked?

One of the first known man-made optical illusions can be found in the Parthenon. This giant temple was built more than 2,400 years ago in the ancient Greek city of Athens. The Parthenon's builders wanted their temple to be one thing above all: impressively beautiful. And beautiful it is … in fact, it is simply perfect. The beams seem to lie perfectly flat, or horizontal, upon the straight columns. Everything about the building is as it appears … or is it?

Yet in reality, nothing here is straight, vertical, or horizontal! The steps are rounded, the columns stand slightly curved, and no one stone is the same as another. These "crooked" parts, however, are arranged in a way that makes the entire building appear completely straight.

Read about it on page 77.

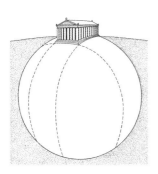

The "crooked" Parthenon

The temple rests upon a curved surface, shaped like a section of a giant ball. If you were to complete the ball, it would have a diameter of about:
a) 100 yards   b) 400 yards   c) 6 miles

During the 1600's in what is now Vatican City, a famous architect was given the job of redesigning a grand stairway called the Scala Regia. This stairway led from the palace of the pope to the giant church of St. Peter's. The available space was narrow and poorly lit, and the artist was supposed to design a stairway fit for the majesty of a pope. What was he to do? The architect reached into his bag of optical tricks. He placed columns along the stairs; each column slightly shorter than the one below it. He also gradually increased the distance between the columns as he went farther up the stairs. These optical tricks make the staircase appear much larger than it really is.

Gian Lorenzo Bernini,
Scala Regia, 1663.
Vatican, Rome

35

Andrea Mantegna, *Camera degli Sposi*, around 1474. Palazzo Ducale, Mantua

Painted worlds, colorful dreams ...

What would a room be like if it had a hole in the ceiling? Unthinkable! And what if that hole had a view into the endlessness of the sky, and into another world? Would this be possible? It would with paint ...

Probably no architect would become famous if he or she left a hole in the ceiling or built a church without a roof. But a painter could. With paint and a few optical tricks, painters can make the impossible possible.

Read about it on page 77.

How many angels ...
. . . . like these two can you find in the large picture on the left?

And what would a church be like without a dome? When the church of Sant'Ignazio in Rome was being built, there wasn't enough money left for the dome. So they simply painted one. In addition to the painted dome, the same painter even "removed" the roof of the church—at least this is how it appears—so visitors could see up into the sky. You can see what this looks like by turning the page.

Andrea Pozzo,
Dome Painting, 1691–94.
Sant'Ignazio, Rome

It's hard to say just where the painted columns and stone of the building ends …

… and where the painted heavens begin.

Andrea Pozzo,
Ceiling Fresco, 1691–94.
Sant'Ignazio, Rome

Raise the curtain and find mysterious spaces!

Is that a curtain we see in the picture below, or is it a brick wall? And what is that purple checkered thing floating in the long, vaulted room? It looks as if it were held up by some ghostly hand! Is it a picture? Is it a space? Is it a dream?

Read about it on page 78.

Do you have an idea?

Is it ...

a)   ... a photomontage?

b)   ... a see-through pane of glass with purple checkers, hanging from transparent cords?

c)   ... a picture made of purple light cast on the walls?

d)   ... a painting on light-colored stone?

Banksy, Graffiti in Hoxton, London

Felice V
Huit carrés, 2
Orang
Palace of Vers

Who's there?

The daughter of the house is allowed to wish the guests a quick good night. And it's no wonder that she's filled with curiosity as she opens the door: beautiful music is being played and people are laughing and dancing. She looks around, curious. The two ladies on the second floor are also looking spellbound at all the guests. Even the dog is obedient today and doesn't move from his spot …

Paolo Veronese, *Hall of Olympus* in the Villa Barbaro Giacomelli, detail, around 1560. Maser (Veneto)

Read about it on page 80.

Make your own "trompe l'oeil"* with you in the leading role!

*A "trompe l'oeil" is a painted picture that tries to make the viewer believe something is there that's really not.

Paolo Veronese, *Hall of Olympus* in the Villa Barbaro Giacomelli, detail, around 1560. Maser (Veneto)

The Barbaro family built a beautiful country house near Venice, Italy, about 440 years ago. People who visited the house for the first time were astonished to discover that not all the guests were "real." Neither were all the columns, balconies, and landscapes. Many of them were, in fact, paintings! And they were painted so that, in candlelight, it was barely possible to tell the difference between the real and the unreal. Great fun for everyone! Just like the painter, Paolo Veronese, had imagined his work would be as he created it.

M. C. Escher,
Belvedere, 1958.
Lithograph

Any three-dimensional object—like a cube—has a front and a back. But how often can you see the front and back of that object change without turning it around? Look carefully at this drawing of a cube.

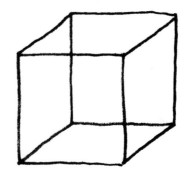

The front of the cube can become the back, and the back can become the front.

The man in the picture, by the way, is looking at the same drawing. He has discovered something surprising while looking … As soon as he looks at the front face of the cube, it changes into the back face; and vice versa.

"Magic" cube
To solve the puzzle, do the following … Make a copy of the two drawings of a cube. On the first one, color the whole front side with a black marker; on the second one, color the entire back side. Do you notice anything?

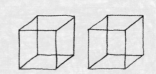

Read about it on page 78.

The magic door
Everything is possible on paper, but how would a magic door function with pieces of Lego? That's easy. Once you know the trick, you can even build the magic door yourself …

Read about it on page 88.

Georges Seurat, *A Sunday Afternoon on the Island of La Grande Jatte*, 1884. Art Institute, Chicago

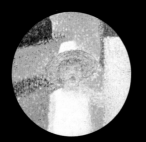

Tricks with color

Red is red and blue is blue? If you think you can believe your eyes when you see a color, then guess again ...

Our eyes can be easily and quickly fooled, even when it's a question of color. It doesn't matter which colored object we look at, we never see only the one color. We always perceive all the surrounding colors as well.

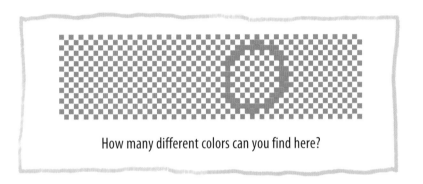

How many different colors can you find here?

Read about it on page 78.

Some painters used this knowledge in their pictures. If they needed to make the color brown, for example, they wouldn't make it the normal way by mixing red and green paint. Instead, they would paint small dots of red and green next to each other on the canvas. They knew that because the red and green points were so close together, they would appear brown in the viewer's eye. The artists used this technique for all the colors in their artworks. Over time, they came to be known as "pointillists."

Read about it on page 78.

One of these six details is not from the painting on the left. Can you find it?

 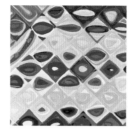  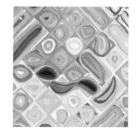

M   A   E   M

*Read about it
on page
78.*

Can you find these details in the picture to the right? If you arrange them as they appear in the picture, from left to right, then the letters will spell out the name of the child.

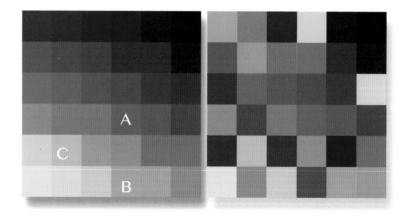

*Read about it
on page
78.*

It´s all in the mix

When one color is placed next to a very different one, then both will change a little bit in shade. This happens because, in the human eye, the colors become mixed with each other and with the surrounding colors. Can you find the colors labeled A, B, and C in the square to the right?

Chuck Clos
Emma, 200
Japanese woodc

48

Giuseppe Arcimboldo, *The Vegetable Gardner*, around 1590. Museo Civico, Cremona

Hidden images and picture puzzles

Unambiguously ambiguous! Get out your detective skills! This is the case of a picture within a picture—and top secret messages!

Delicious ... these carrots, onions, mushrooms ... but who is that peeping strangley out from the vegetables? Can you see the funny face? Turn the picture upside down and you´ll see!

When Giuseppe Arcimboldo painted this picture more than four hundred years ago, it had been common practice for painters to represent nature in a very realistic and detailed way. But Arcimboldo wanted more. On the one hand, he wanted to paint what he saw in front of him. But on the other hand, he wanted to surprise the viewers of his paintings with something mysterious and unexpected. Did he succeed?

What happens when you turn the monkey and the smiling face upside down? What was hidden becomes visible! But wait … Even before you turn the pictures upside down, can you imagine what they will look like? What will you see? It's not so easy, is it?

Secret messages

Two men, a curtain, a table, many strange things …

But what is this? At the very front of the picture stretches some strange object that can't be made out at all, even though the artist painted everything else so clearly.

Read about it on page 78.

What is hidden here?

If you want to solve this hidden riddle, you can't look at this picture the way you usually look at pictures! Instead, try putting the right side of your nose along the little arrow and look in the direction of the strange object. Suddenly it changes into a … Can you see it?

Distorted images like these are called anamorphoses, or "re-formations." They once were used to encode secret messages. Only if you knew how to look could you solve the riddle, recognize the picture, and then—usually—understand the message.

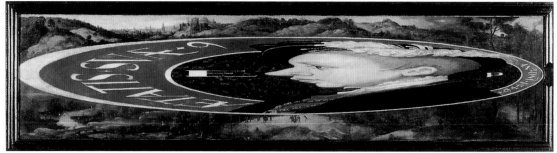

William Scrots, *Portrait of Edward, Prince of Wales*, 1546. National Portrait Gallery, London

It used to be popular to change the faces of famous people by means of anamorphoses like these.

Read about it on page 79.

Encode your own message …

… with the help of an anamorphosis. How does it work?
Look to the right.

Hans Holbein the younger, *The Ambassadors*, 1533. National Portrait Gallery, London

A visit to the cabinet of mirrors ...

A mirror is a mysterious thing. How can an object appear as an image in the mirror when in reality it is in front of the mirror?

And where exactly is this reflected image, on the surface of the mirror? Or behind it? Which is the real and which the unreal world?

For a long time, mirrors were believed to be windows into another world. "Mirrors lie, appearances deceive," goes an old saying. In other words, the image that is reflected in the mirror is not reality itself, but an unreal and deceptive appearance.

Lucas Furtenagel, *The Painter Hans Burgkmair and His Wife Anna*, 1527. Kunsthistorisches Museum, Vienna

"Mirror, mirror in the hand…" The two don't look exactly happy— no wonder, when you consider what they see in the mirror.

Read about it on page 79.

A mirror image: only a deception?

Look at yourself in the mirror and touch your left hand to your left ear. In the mirror you see something different, namely your right hand touching your right ear!

Try this experiment: look at your face in a mirror and mark two points from your face on the mirror (maybe your hairline and your chin) with a water-soluble marker. Measure how far apart the two points are in the mirror and in reality. Do you notice anything?

René Magritte, *Not To Be Reproduced*, 1937. Museum Boijmans Van Beuningen, Rotterdam

A picture in a picture in a picture ...

Some time ago, a young art researcher went before the public and explained that this picture by the painter Robert Campin shows more than just a young woman. If you look more closely at the ring on her finger, he claimed, you can see the face of a bearded man in it: a self-portrait of the painter, thought the young researcher.

Other scholars, who had known this picture for years and had never seen the tiny portrait, thought this discovery was pure fantasy and explained it as an optical illusion. What do you think: spot of color or face?

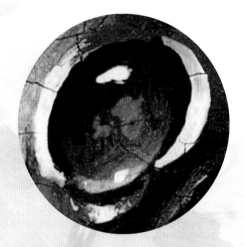

In fact, our eyes constantly try to read meaning into things that don't make any sense ... just like in the case of this ring, perhaps.

You can try this out yourself with inkblots, for example.

Read about it on page 87.

Make your own inkblot pictures!

Robert Camp
A Woman, 144
National Gallery, Lond

Eye test for advanced students

What do you see in these pictures?

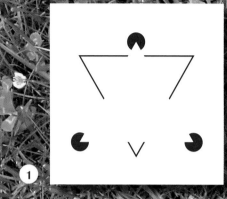

1

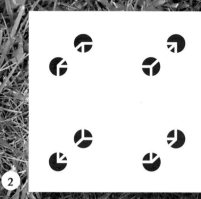

2

3

4

Read about it
on page
79.

5

6

And here?

Does it show people coming in, or a portrait of a long-haired man? Perhaps both?

Salvador Dalí, *Disappearing Bust of Voltaire*, 1941.

M.C. Escher, *Waterfall*, 1961. Lithograph

That can't be!

The impossible becomes possible.
Enter the "fun fair of impossible things"!

"Paper is patient." What this saying means is that on paper everything is possible, whether written, drawn, or painted. Even things and structures that can't actually exist in reality can look real on paper or canvas and can really confuse our eyes.

M.C. Escher,
Möbius strip II (Red Ants), 1963.
Woodcut

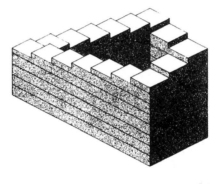

*Read about it
on page
79.*

Impossible or not?
Look at the pictures on these two pages again more carefully.
Something isn't right. Can you see what it is?
a) picture, p. 60: Can water flow like this?
b) picture to the left: Can ants walk endlessly on a figure 8?
c) picture above: Are there stairs on which you can keep going up
or down endlessly?

Did you solve the puzzle? Then you already know that one of the three pictures is not an optical Illusion. One of the three structures just looks crazy, but it's not. And you can even build it yourself!

*Read about it
on page
88.*

Art on art on art ...

This artist doesn't need any paints for his art, but he uses what is already there. Thousands of images from a computer, placed closely together, can create a completely new work of art. Look at this detail more closely!

New and old

What you see here is not really so new at all. Do you recognize this lady?
Here's a hint: Compare this picture with the one on page 23!

Squint for a moment. Do you notice anything? Our eyes can mix colors. Do you remember the "pointillist" painter on page 47 and what he realized?
This artist's work is made in the same way, with only one small difference. He uses the help of his computer to achieve the perfect result.

Robert Silvers, *Mona Lisa*, 2002.

Just what's going on here?

If you were to step into this picture and walk around, you would soon become completely

bewildered. Can you see why?

Around 250 years ago, the English artist William Hogarth made this engraving*. In it, he poked

fun at all those artists who made mistakes of perspective in their paintings and drawings.

*In an engraving, lines are carved into a copper plate and then filled with ink. The ink is then wiped off the
surface so that it remains only in the carved lines. The plate is then printed on paper.

*Read about it
on page
79.*

This funny picture shows just how important correct perspective is. William
Hogarth put numerous mistakes into his engraving. You can see a few examples
above. Do you see what's wrong with each of them?

William Hogarth, *Satire on False Perspective*, 1753. The British Museum, London

"I see it differently than you,"

you may have heard someone say before. And in fact, several people can look at one and the same object or picture and see very different things.

Picture puzzle with Mary and Jesus, 19th century.
Schwäbisches Bauernhofmuseum, Illerbeuren

If two people stand in front of the picture shown below, each one will see something different. The person looking at the picture from the left will see a bearded Jesus, while the one looking from the right will see Mary. Then both can say at once, "I see something you don't see!" This kind of picture is called a perspectival double portrait.

Make your own perspectival double portrait

Would you like to make a picture like this yourself? You could use pictures that you paint yourself, or you could use photographs. It makes a great gift!

Read about it on page 87.

Round and round—on the carousel of art …

Here everything revolves around art, and everything in art is revolving too. If you're not careful, you'll be revolving as well …

Art that moves … Moving images made up of paint, brushstrokes, and a canvas? How is that supposed to work?

Painters who wanted to portray their surroundings in a realistic way could not avoid painting a moving object every now and then: a dog running, a wheel turning...

Around 1650 the Spanish artist Diego Velázquez devised an ingenious method for his painting *The Spinners*. Instead of painting each separate spoke of the spinning wheel, he painted a blurred round surface.

1

2

How does movement enter the picture? "Why is the flower pot floating in the air?," you might wonder about picture 1. But in picture 2, the flowerpot is clearly flying through the air. Why?

Read about it on page 79.

Read about it on page 79.

Get your picture moving!
In the creative projects section you will find a similar picture, which you can photocopy, "set in motion" with a few simple changes, and glue into the box to the right.

Read about it on page 83.

Read about it on page 83.

go Velázquez,
Spinners, around 1657.
eo del Prado, Madrid

William Turner, *Rain, Steam, Speed*, 1844. National Gallery, London

Now you see it, now you don't!

With the invention of the train around 200 years ago, "movement" and "speed" started to become the subjects of paintings. For these new kinds of pictures, artists had to think up completely new techniques. How is it possible to paint speed and movement?

Read about it on page 83.

Get moving! Build yourself a "thaumatrope"!

To achieve a little movement in your pictures, you'll need something called a thaumatrope, or "wonder turner." But what is a thaumatrope?

Lights, camera, action!

When the first movie was shown around 100 years ago, people were thrilled. "Pictures can move!," they thought about the sensational invention. But it wasn't painters who had achieved this miracle; photographers had done it. They made countless individual photos—each one was only slightly different from the previous one. The pictures were then shown so quickly one after the other that they appeared to the eye like flowing movement.

Some painters incorporated this new discovery into their paintings. Giacomo Balla painted his "dachshund with 100 legs" in 1912. Not only do his legs seem to move; but you can also see his happily wagging tail, his flying ears, and the swinging of his leash!

Giacomo Balla, *Dynamism of a Dog on a Leash*, 1912. Museum of Modern Art, New York

Flip book
Would you also like to "generate movement" by making one picture merge into the next? Try it out with a flip book.

Read about it on page 80.

Flickering pictures in black and white

Around forty years ago, a number of artists thought that two-dimensional and non-moving pictures were incredibly old-fashioned. They thought that art should be like a modern person: moving, changing, entertaining. They achieved these qualities by building optical tricks into their pictures.

This kind of art was given the name "Op-Art," short for Optical Art. Many works by Op-Art artists ran on batteries and really did move. But many others were completely two-dimensional and painted only in back and white. By means of optical tricks and illusions alone, these two-dimensional paintings created the impression of movement—and often unbelievable depth.

* *Two-dimensional refers to everything flat. In contrast; bodies, globes, and other objects that have depth are three-dimensional.

Wanted: Op-Art artists!
You can see just how bewildering black and white can be when you do this experiment.

*Read about it
on page
85.*

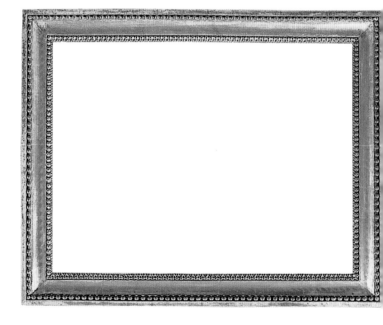

Bridget Riley, *Blaze 4*, 1964. Private collection

Eye test for connoisseurs

Test your eye—see your score

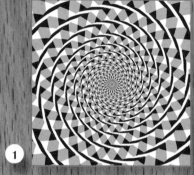

1 What shapes do the lines in this picture make: circles or spirals?

2 How many light blue dots do you see on the white frame between the blue squares?

3 Is the yellow star in the upper or lower half of the red triangle?

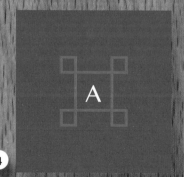

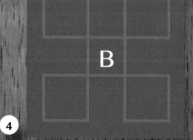

4 **4** Which square is smaller, A or B? Or are they both the same size?

5 Can you find Napoleon's ghost?

6 Where is the lady with the hat?

7 Where is the old man's head?

8 Where is the girl hiding?

Score:

8 correct answers: Wow! What's up with your eyes?

3 – 7 correct answers: Great, you understand the tricks

0 – 2 correct answers: Don't worry, that's completely normal!

Read about it on page 79.

Solutions

Real or painted? (page 8)

Parrhasius was considered the greatest artist. Zeuxis may have fooled animals, but Parrhasius fooled Zeuxis!

Eye test for beginners: Original and deception (pages 10–11)

The photographs are numbers 3, 4, 7, and 10.

Test your perception (page 13)

Incredible but true: the two orange circles are exactly the same. In the picture on the left, the orange circle appears small because we compare it to the larger gray circles. On the right, it appears large because the circles around it are small.

Optical illusion: Do it yourself (page 14)

In order to produce an optical illusion like this, you have to arrange two familiar objects together in a photograph so that they appear to touch each other. One of the objects needs to be much closer to the camera than the other object. The closer one will appear unusually large, like the arm shown here.

Eclipse and the moon (page 14)

Answer b) is right.

What is the sky really like? (page 15)

Stars are enormous spheres. But despite this, we generally see them and paint them with points. Why? The human eye is actually not one piece, but it consists of six segments. Thus when the eye sees a brightly lit, far-away object—such as a star—the light from that object can appear slightly broken up. This broken-up, or refracted, light can cause our eyes to see the stars with points.

And neither is the sky really blue! As it enters the atmosphere, the white light of the sun is broken down into the separate colors that make it up. During the day the light shines upon the Earth almost vertically, so that only the shorter wavelengths of light reach the Earth. We see these shorter light waves as blue. When the sun sinks towards the horizon, only the longer wavelengths reach the Earth. We often see this light as red, as in the evening sky.

How does an artist paint the Holy Spirit? (page 18)

The Holy Spirit is painted in the form of a dove.

Real or not? (page 21)

The details of real people are in the lower row to the left and right.

Mona Lisa—Here's looking at you ... (page 22)

Answer a) is right.

The trick with the glance (page 24)

The lady on the right is no longer looking at you, even though her eyes remain unchanged. Strange, isn't it? The figure's gaze is determined by more than just the eyes, it is also determined by the direction of the nose, the position of the head, and so on.

Eye test for clever viewers: Magic eyes (page 26)

To find the hidden image in the magic picture, you have to be able to look at it "out of focus." Here's how ... Hold the picture about one foot in front of your eyes. Don´t look at it as you would normally look at a picture, but try to look through it. Imagine that you are trying to focus on a point just behind the picture. If you can do this, then the following might happen: Your eyes suddenly see a three-dimensional image within the picture. It is not entirely easy to see this, and only a few viewers are able to do it right away. So keep trying! You'll eventually be able to see a rabbit in the picture.

Eye test for clever viewers: From fair to foul (page 27)

If you turn the picture of the young lady upside-down, you immediately see why she should stay as she was. Not all of her face had been upside-down—her eyes and mouth had not been changed—and now her whole face looks very strange. But as long as you look at the picture of the young woman upside-down, you don't notice this odd alteration. This is because when our eyes perceive a face, they always perceive its individual parts: mouth, nose, eyes—and these all appear to be just fine. We notice the terrible distortion only when we turn the picture around. To the right, you can see how the picture is hung in the museum.

Big, bigger, biggest ... (page 30)

The three funny men are exactly the same size, of course. The one in the "back" of the picture seems much larger than the one in the "front" or the one in the "middle." This is an optical illusion. We perceive the man in the background to be farther away from us than the other two men. In real life, people and objects appear smaller to us if they are farther away. Thus if a painter wants to make people look the same size, he or she has to make the people in the background smaller than those in the foreground. Because the man in the back of this painting is, in reality, the same size as the men in the foreground, our brain concludes that this "far-away" figure must be enormous.

J.A.D. Ingres, *Mademoiselle Caroline Rivière*, 1805. Musee du Louvre, Paris

A line on the wall (page 31)

B surely seems longer to you, doesn't it? But it's not; in fact, both lines are exactly the same length.

The "crooked" Parthenon (page 35)

Answer c) is right.

How many angels can you find? (page 37)

Ten angels are hidden in this heavenly scene.

Raise the curtain and find mysterious spaces ... (page 40)

This mysterious space is a painting on light-colored stone. If you look at the painting from a different angle than the one intended by the painter, you can see how he created the optical illusion.

"Magic" cube (page 45)

At first it's not so easy to decide which side of the cube is the front and which is the back. As soon as you paint one of the sides black, it appears like the front side ... even if you saw it as the back before.

Using a drawing of a cube like this, the man in the picture has built something strange and impossible: a cube-like object in which the front side is simultaneously the back side. But of course this only works on paper ...

How many different colors can you find here? (page 47)

In this drawing, there is only one shade of red and one shade of green! The red spots that are next to green ones appear to the viewer's eyes like a mixture of red and green: brown. The red spots near the white ones appear to be a brighter shade of red.

Find the detail (page 47)

The detail on the left side of page 47 is not from the Seurat painting.

What's the name of the child? (page 48)

The child's name is E-M-M-A.

It's all in the mix (page 48)

When looking at colors, too, the brain is guided by the surroundings. A color looks very different when placed next to a differently-colored neighbor. The colored squares A, B, and C can be found in the picture to the right in the places marked. Are they where you thought they would be?

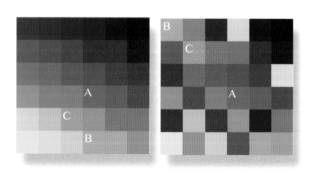

What's hidden here? (page 52)

When you look at it from the side, the strange blotch in the picture is transformed into a skull.

Encode your own message . . . (page 52)

The encoded word is: SECRET

To make your own secret message, draw each letter of your message as tall as possible. If you then tilt the page and look at the letters from the same angle as you did in our example, then you'll be able to read the text.

A mirror image: Only a deception? (page 54)

Every mirror image shows its reflected object exactly half as large as it really is.

Eye test for advanced students: what do you see in these pictures? (page 58)

1. A white triangle with one of its tips pointing straight up. Even though there's no such white triangle in the first drawing, our eyes fill one in because the black circles are arranged in a way that hint at that form. If you cover up the black circles, this triangle disappears.

2. A cube. Here too our eyes fill in something that's not there. Even though many of the white lines are not visible, our eyes connect them up to make the shape of a cube.

3. A vase and two faces can be seen here.

4. What was old becomes young again and vice versa: do you see an old woman or a young woman?

5. Duck or rabbit?

6. Oops, this elephant's legs have gotten all mixed up. Can you help sort them out?

Impossible or not? (page 61)

The pictures (a) and (c) are impossible. Picture (b) is possible!

Just what's going on here? (page 64)

The mistakes in perspective are marked here.

How does movement enter the picture? (page 69)

In picture 2, the artist added some lines that give the impression that the flower pot has created a draft of air and is flying.

Eye test for connoisseurs (pages 74–75)

1. They are circles! Trace them with a pen or your finger.
2. There aren´t any light blue dots between the blue squares.
3. The star is exactly in the center of the triangle.
4. Both squares are exactly the same size.

5

6

7

8

Great creative projects

Here are lots of instructions for creative projects. If you don't want to cut up the book, you can make photocopies of the pictures.

Get some perspective (page 31) Join point A with A, B with B, and C with C.

A •

B •

• A
• B
• C

C •

Make your own trompe l'oeil with you in the leading role! (page 42)

What you need: 1. a simple picture frame (without glass), 2. scissors and glue, 3. a photo of yourself in which you are reaching around a door frame and your hands and arms are clearly visible. When the picture is finished, it's going to look like you're trying to break out of the picture frame . . . so make an appropriate facial expression. Here's what to do:

1. Print (or have printed) two copies of the photograph that are just large enough to fit in the picture frame. It should be just big enough so that when it's framed, the hands are covered by the frame.

2. Frame the photo.

3. Cut the hands out from the second photo and glue them to the outside of the frame. If your hair is long, you can also cut out a few strands of hair from the second photo and glue them onto the frame too.

Make your own flip book (page 71)

To make pictures "really" move, you can create a flip book. For this you'll need a small notebook with around 30 or 40 sheets. Using a pen or pencil, draw a small picture on each sheet—making sure that each new picture is only slightly different from the one before it. If you want to show a sunrise, for example; first draw only the horizon, then a small section of the sun, then a bit more of the sun, and so on. Only after many drawings should the sun be high up in the sky. Even if you can't draw very well, you can still "shoot" a little film by making a small dot jump around on the notebook pages.

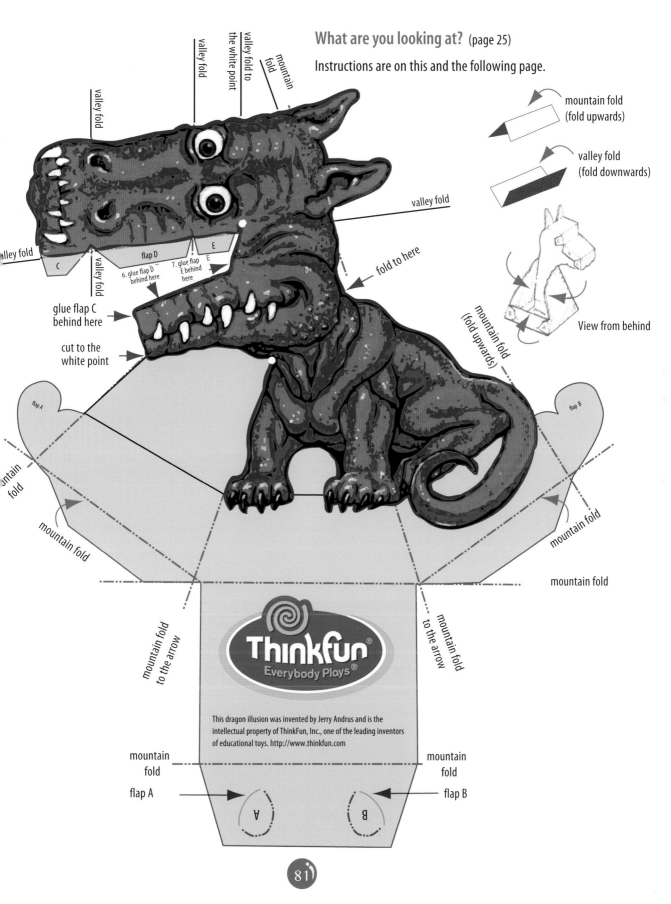

Instructions are on this and the following page.

mountain fold
(fold upwards)

valley fold
(fold downwards)

valley fold

valley fold

valley fold to
the white point

mountain
fold

valley fold

fold to here

flap D

E

6. glue flap D
behind here

7. glue flap
E behind
here

E

mountain fold
(fold upwards)

View from behind

glue flap C
behind here

cut to the
white point

C

valley fold

valley fold

flap A

flap B

mountain
fold

mountain fold

mountain fold

mountain fold

mountain fold

mountain fold
to the arrow

mountain fold
to the arrow

Thinkfun®
Everybody Plays®

This dragon illusion was invented by Jerry Andrus and is the
intellectual property of ThinkFun, Inc., one of the leading inventors
of educational toys. http://www.thinkfun.com

mountain
fold

mountain
fold

flap A

flap B

A

B

81

The eyes of a dragon are following you:

You will need only scissors, glue, and the pattern on the previous page.

Make the small paper dragon as described.

Cut him out and glue together where marked. Make sure that you fold it as described: the head has to curve inwards, not outwards! Put your paper figure in a well-lit place. If you stand a yard or two away from the paper dragon and move back and forth or up and down, it will appear as if he´s moving his head. When you do this, squint your eyes. Can you see how he follows you with his eyes?

Have fun with your new pet!

Get moving! Build yourself a "thaumatrope"! (page 70)

To add a little movement to your pictures, you'll need a thaumatrope—a "wonder turner." To make one, you can use the two round drawings on the back of this page. You'll also need some cardboard; a thin, smooth wooden stick; tape; and glue. Brightly color the two drawings, glue them onto the cardboard, and cut them out. Use the tape to fasten the stick to the back of one of the drawings, so that it sticks out from the bottom of the drawing in the middle.

Then glue the other drawing to the first one, so that the two pictures appear on opposite sides. The whole thing should look like a large lollipop. Now twirl the wooden stick rapidly between the palms of your hands. What happens?

Get your picture moving! (page 69)

Add a few lines behind the kangaroo, making sure the lines go slightly upward from left to right, and the animal hops away ...

Living faces (page 17)

drawing I   drawing II

 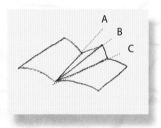

Here's how it works ... Fold the photo of the young lady on the back of this page as shown in drawing I. Fold A runs through the pupil of the left eye and through a corner of the mouth; fold C does the same thing on the other side of the face. Fold B runs down the nose and through the center of the mouth. The picture should look like the sheet in drawing II. Now look at the young lady from below and above: she's smiling at you!

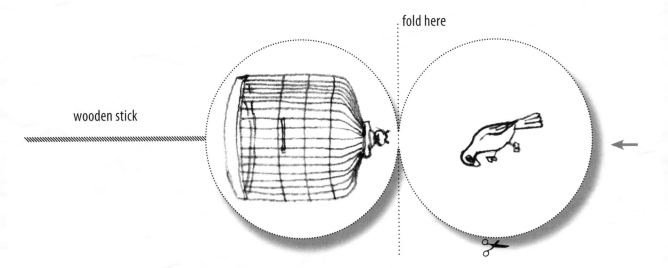

wooden stick

fold here

Leonardo da Vinci, *Portrait of Gineva de'Benci*, around 1480.
National Gallery of Art, Washington

Build your own perspective box (page 32)

You'll need a ruler, scissors, glue, and colored pencils or pens. Cut out the sheet on the back of this page and fold over the edges using the ruler and the pointed tip of the scissors. Before you glue the box together where it's marked, you can color it any way you like. For example, you can create dark and light squares. When you look into the peep-show, make sure that your eyes are at the level of the horizon. The picture in the box shows an old city street ... a street that looks like it goes on forever!

· ✂

Wanted: Op-Art artists! (page 72)

Cut out the picture on the back of this page. It looks a little bit like a brick wall. Then color all the rectangles marked with black dots. The others rectangles should stay white.

Do the horizontal lines still look horizontal? Or have you just created a great optical trick? You can glue your finished artwork into the frame on page 72.

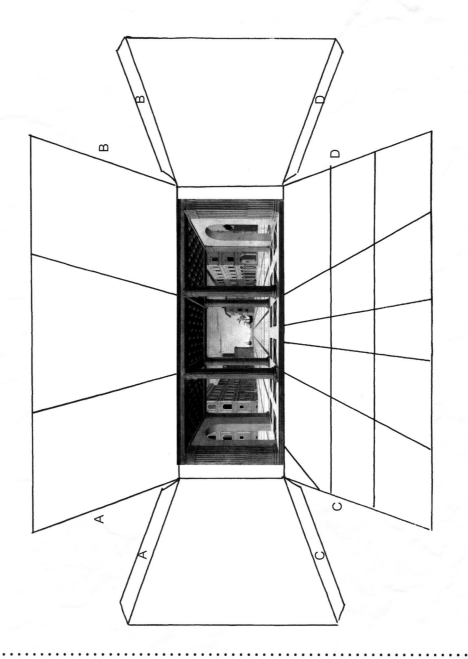

Make your own inkblot pictures (page 56)

All you need is paper and a box of watercolors.

Here's how it works ... Fold a sheet of paper once in the middle and open it again. Then drip as many spots of paint as you like on the paper. If you now fold the two sides of the paper together, then all the areas of paint imprint themselves onto the other side as well. A fantastical image emerges.

So, what can you see in your inkblot picture?

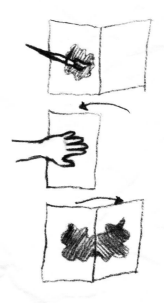

Make your own perspectival double portrait (page 67)

What you need:

– one 8 ½ x 11 sheet of white paper

– two sheets half that size (simply cut an 8 ½ x 11 sheet in half)

– colored pens or pencils, paints, or two copies of photographs the same size as the half sheets

– a glue stick

Fold the large sheet of paper in half by bringing the two short sides together. Repeat twice until you get a thick, narrow strip of paper. Now unfold the sheet. Your sheet should have eight narrow sections separated by seven folds.

Now lay the two smaller sheets vertically and paint them. Fold these sheets, too, by bringing the long sides together. Then fold once more the same way to create narrow, thick paper strips.

Open up the two smaller painted sheets and cut them along the folds. You should have four strips of picture 1 and four strips of picture 2.

Glue each of the strips onto the narrow sections of the larger sheet ... starting with picture 1. Make sure that you glue the strips in the right order and that you glue them onto every other section. When you are finished, glue the strips of picture 2 onto the remaining sections.

Once the glue has dried, push the entire sheet together a little bit. The folds should stick out, but you should still be able to see all the painted strips. Now look at your sheet from the left and from the right. Can you see the two different images?

glue here

Impossible or not? (page 61)

You can also make a Möbius Strip. An ant could walk along this structure without ever coming to an edge. Cut out the strip of paper to the left—or a photocopy of it—and glue the two ends together so that the two hearts are exactly on top of each other. To do this, you will have to twist the strip so that it makes an 8. You can see how this strip never ends when you move the tip of a pencil along your finished structure.

The magic door of Lego (page 45)

You will need nine Lego bricks with two knobs each, one Lego beam eight knobs long, a small Lego base, one Lego figure, and a camera.

The figure faces this direction.

Take your picture diagonally from this direction and from above.

First, construct a tower of five two-knob Lego blocks and put the thin beam on top. Build a second tower of the same width, but only four blocks high. These towers should be placed as shown in the diagram and photo. Then place the figure as shown so that it faces the long beam. Finally, take a photograph of your structure … making sure that the beam looks like it's resting on the second tower.

glue here